SANT BISHAN SINGH MURALEWALE

ISHWAR SINGH

I am dedicating this book to the selfless sewa of Sant Bishan Singh Muralewale.

Contents

Foreword

Ishwar Singh have more than ten years of experience in writing story books, sakhis of devotional saints and in research activities. He is a tremendous writer. He is doing excellent job by writing about Sant Bishan Singh Muralewale. He had shown very keen interest in the field of religious resources and other cultural issues.

He is also a very excellent teacher and also having deep knowledge about the social science issues. I have always seen him working very hard for his various books. He just want to express about the Indian culture to our new generations in a simple and brief manner. I wish him all the very best for his new book.

Birinder Pal Kaur

Preface

This book is about the brief history of Sant Bishan Singh Muralewale. The task behind to publish such content is to spread knowledge about the unsung heroes of the Sikh history among the new generation. In the schools, which are being organised by Sikh trusts, the students are just getting very limited knowledge about the Sikh warriors. Baba Banda Singh Bahadur, Baba Deep Singh etc. are the common names on the tongues of the students but they don't know about the others. This is just an effort to spread this brief information among new generations. I hope that you will like this book.

Acknowledgements

Writing a book is harder than I thought and more rewarding than I could have ever imagined. None of this would have been possible without my best friend, my teacher, my best motivator, my beloved mother Amarjit Kaur. She was the first who inspired me for my goals and taught me various subjects and created my interest specially in Social Sciences. She stood by me during every struggle and all my successes. Whatever I had achieved in my life it is due to my mother.

I'm eternally grateful to my father Pal Singh, who took in an extra mouth to feed when he didn't have to. He taught me discipline, tough love, manners, respect, and so much more that has helped me succeed in life. I truly have no idea where I'd be if he hadn't given me a roof over my head whom I desperately needed at that age.

To my father-in-law Narinder Singh for their moral support during the up and downs in my life. He taught me how to live positive even in the worst situations by sharing his personal experiances. He is the man who suggest me to write a book in your life because it will be your book by which you will be remembered in future.

To Dr. Davinder Singh, who never saw my age, my race, or my lack of formal education. He just saw a kid hungry to learn, hungry to grow, and hungry to succeed in teaching. He never stopped me; he only encouraged me.

Finally, to all those who have been a part of my getting there: Sukhbir Singh, Jarnail Singh, Beant Kaur, Devinder Kumar Sharma, Sumeet Kaur, Rinkpal Singh and Iqbal Singh.

Prologue

India is a country of huge cultural diversities. This diversity has its roots in the ancient and medieval period of the history. In present day life, every one is playing his role according to the role assingned by the nature. I have very much interest to explore various great warriors or personalities and cultural aspects of our Indian Society. So an idea came in my mind to explore the brief history of Sant Bishan Singh Muralewale. In this book, I have focused on the various achievements of Sant Bishan Singh Muralewale. I am writing this book for our younger generations so that when they will read this book, they must understand the sacrifices and struggles of our forefathers.

CHAPTER ONE

Sant Bishan Singh Muralewale

Bohith is the hamlet in the district of Gujrat (now in Pakistan), where Sant Baba Bishan Singh ji Muralewale was born. Sant Ji had a rehat that was very disciplined and was a wonderful scholar. Baba ji was from a sehajdhari Sikh household, which means that they hadn't yet received Amrit. Baba Ji was born in 1852 to Ratna Devi and Lal Dev Ji. As soon as they were born, Baba ji were cleansed before being deposited at the charan/feet of Sri Guru Granth Sahib ji at the Gurdwara. Baba Ji received the gurti (blessings) of Amrit because the Granthi Singh at the Gurdwara performed the birth ceremony in accordance with the rehat maryada of a Gursikh. Following the Ardas, Baba ji received a Hukamnama and was given the name Bishan Singh.

Baba ji remembered Sri Jap ji Sahib ji and learned Gurmukhi by participating in the sangat of other Gursikh Saints. The following ancient holy sites have previously been visited by the 13-year-old Sant Bishan Singh Muralewale: Sri Harmandir Sahib Amritsar, Taran Taaran Sahib, Ganga Parayagraj, Badree Nath Dehradoon Rameshwar Matha, Ayudhia, Nankana Sahib, Dera Sahib

Lahore, and Kiratpur Sahib. The Gursikhs in Amritsar impressed Baba ji when he was 21 years old. They made the decision to take Amrit and join the Khalsa Panth at this point. At Sri Akal Takhat Sahib, they carried this out. Baba ji would meditate on both Gurmantar and Moolmantar for extended periods of time while reciting Gurbani with intense focus. Pandit Tara Singh and Pandit Sadhoo Singh taught them the jog mat, puran, simritian, and grammar of Sanskrit. Baba Ji studied these for nine years.

After that, Baba Ji visited Sant Giani Harnam Singh ji Bedi's sangat. One of Giani Ji's primary sevadars was Baba Ji. Giani ji taught Baba ji all he knew about the Sri Guru Granth Sahib, Sri Dasam Granth Sahib, and the entire history of our Guru Sahibs. Following that, Baba ji was assigned the seva of instructing other Gursikhs and leading the daily Katha.

Baba ji kept him focused on the charan of Akal Purkh for as long as he could. Particularly with their kakaars, he was exceedingly severe in their rehat. Baba Ji avoided the four sins for all time and never even allowed a negative idea to enter his dreams.

The sangat of Murale asked Baba ji to visit Murale and establish a permanent residence there after Sant Ameer Singh ji passed away. About 200 Gurbani students at Murale were preparing to become kathakars, keertanis, and paathis. Among Baba ji's pupils were Sant Giani Sundar Singh ji Bhindranwale, Sant Baba Prem Singh ji Muralewale, and Sant Baba Bhagat Singh ji Ghebewale. An excellent langar was provided for the sangat at all times as part of Seva Baba ji's work in Murale.

At the Amrit vela, Baba ji performs a two-hour Katha. After that, they selected a peaceful location and spend the remainder of the day in intense meditation while attached to the charan of Akal Purkh. Baba ji loves to participate in Seva. Before conducting the daily Katha, Baba ji would fill 150 buckets with water for their pupils' ishnaan once they had completed their ishnaan and nitnem. Baba Ji then finish the Seva of Guru Ji's parkash by cleaning the Gurdwara's floor. Baba ji used to grind fresh flour for degh every day. Sant Giani Sundar Singh ji eventually began to carry out all the seva that Baba ji was undertaking.

At the Gurdwara in Murale, no one was permitted to speak about anything except reciting Gurbani or performing simran of the Gurmantar or Moolmantar. Baba ji only consume a few handful of beans and pulses at a time, along with a small amount of water. They used to do simran for 23 hours every day in order to honour Akal Purkh. A few Gursikhs once requested him to come outside on Diwali night to witness the candles and lights the sangat had ignited since Baba ji led such a nice lifestyle and had attained such a beautiful spiritual condition. Baba ji responded to them as follows: Why do we need to view these lights of the cosmos? Let me stay here and see the light of Waheguru in my heart, the lighter of all of these lights, for many years now instead of looking up to see the ceiling of this room, the moon, the sun, or the stars.

When Sant Baba Sundar Singh Ji was doing tapasaya in kapli asan, Sant Baba Bishan Singh Ji Muralewale came across him while he was out strolling (posture). Sant Ji was standing cross-legged with his feet high in the air and his head pointing down to the ground.

What are you doing, Sant Baba Sundar Singh Ji was questioned by Sant Baba Bishan Singh Ji Muralewale.

"I don't know what to do, but wherever I turn I see Satguru Sri Guru Nanak Dev Ji Maharaj," Sant Baba Sundar Singh Ji retorted. Any way I move my feet, Guru Nanak Dev

Ji is there. I sit in this posture because I'm unsure of where to put my feet.

Sant Baba Bishan Singh Ji Muralewale said, "Your recitation of Sri Jap ji sahib has totally awakened your Dib Drishtee (celestial vision), and Dhan Dhan Sri Guru Nanak Dev Ji Maharaj is immensely happy."

Sant Giani Sundar Singh ji, who was totally versed in the knowledge of Gurbani and was permanently disciplined in Gursikh rehat, was chosen as the next Jathedar of Damdami Taksal before Baba ji ascended to Sach Khand. At the age of 53 and following the bhog of an Akhand Paath Baba ji, he left this world for Sach Khand in the year 1905.